ART & DESIGN CAREERS

A Career in FILM AND VIDEO

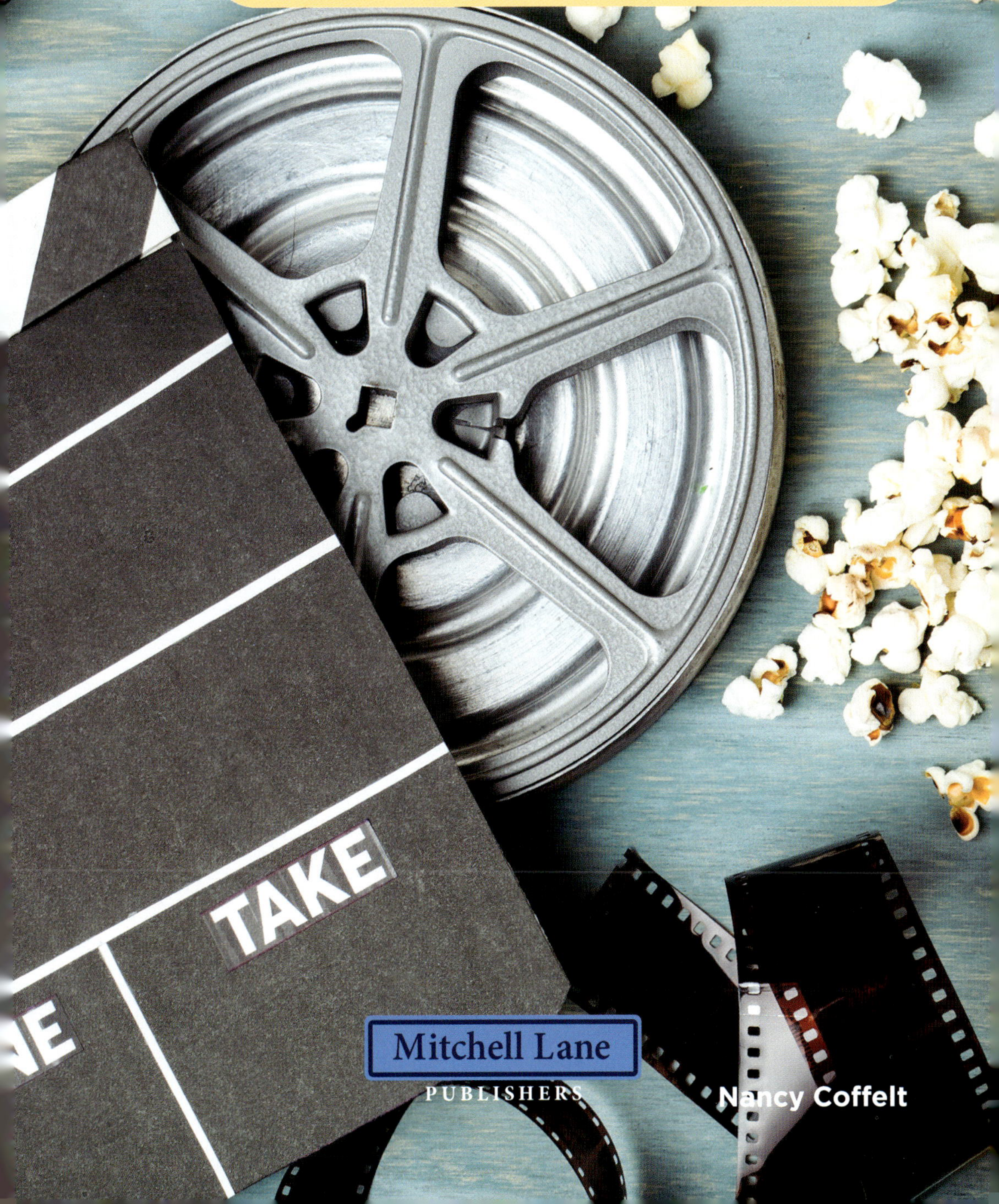

Nancy Coffelt

Mitchell Lane PUBLISHERS

Mitchell Lane
PUBLISHERS

mitchelllanepub.com

2001 SW 31st Avenue
Hallandale, FL 33009

First Edition, 2026.
Author: Nancy Coffelt
Designer: Ed Morgan
Editor: Tammy Gagne

Series: Art and Design Careers
Title: A Career in Film and Video

Library bound ISBN: 979-8-89260-501-4
eBook ISBN: 979-8-89260-509-0

Photo credits: cover, contents, p. 5, 7, 9, 11, 15, 21 freepik.com; p. 13, 31 wikimedia; p. 17, 19, 23, 27 Alamy; p. 25, 29, 33, 35, 37, 41, 43 Shutterstock

Contents

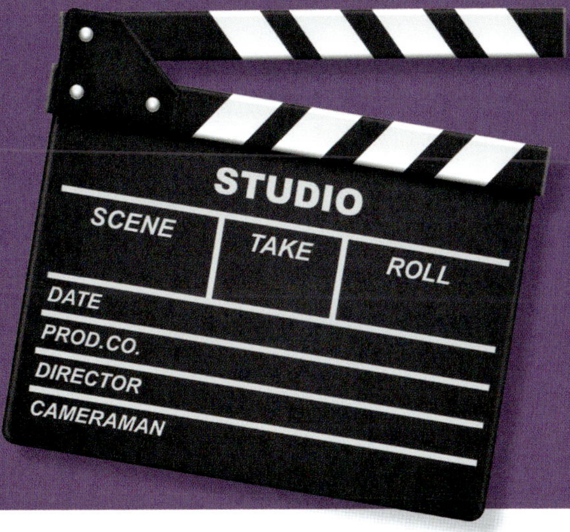

Chapter One

Another Form of Storytelling

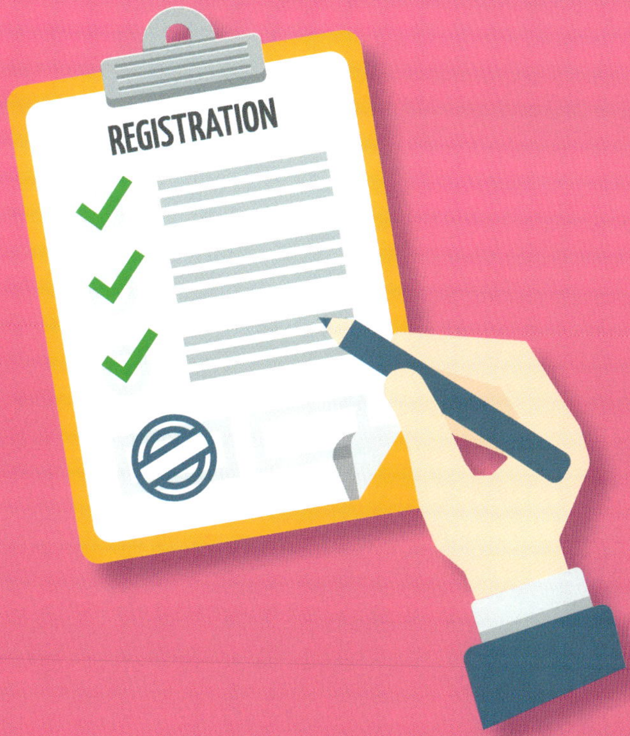

"I'm sorry," said the volunteer at the summer arts program's front desk. "The class on writing graphic novels is full."

"Oh, no," Josh groaned. He had an idea for an exciting graphic novel. His two main characters find a mysterious book. Each time they open it, they can see one day into the future. Josh had been looking forward to the graphic novel class ever since he'd first heard about it. "I guess I'll call my dad to come back and get me," he said. He dug his phone out of his pocket to make the call.

CHAPTER ONE

"Hey, Josh!" He turned to see his friend Raven waving to him. She had been in his creative writing class at school. "I am so excited for this class," she told him as she got closer.

"It's full," Josh replied. "I couldn't get in."

Raven seemed puzzled. She pointed to a signup sheet on the table. "No, it's not. Look, there are two more spots open."

Josh looked down. The phrase *Learning Film and Video* was printed across the top of a bright blue piece of paper. "Oh, I'm not here for that class," he said.

"Why not?" Raven asked. "It's going to be great."

"But you like to write stories," Josh pointed out.

"I do," Raven said. "And now I'm going to learn a whole new way to tell them. Take the class with me."

"I don't know anything about making films or videos," Josh said.

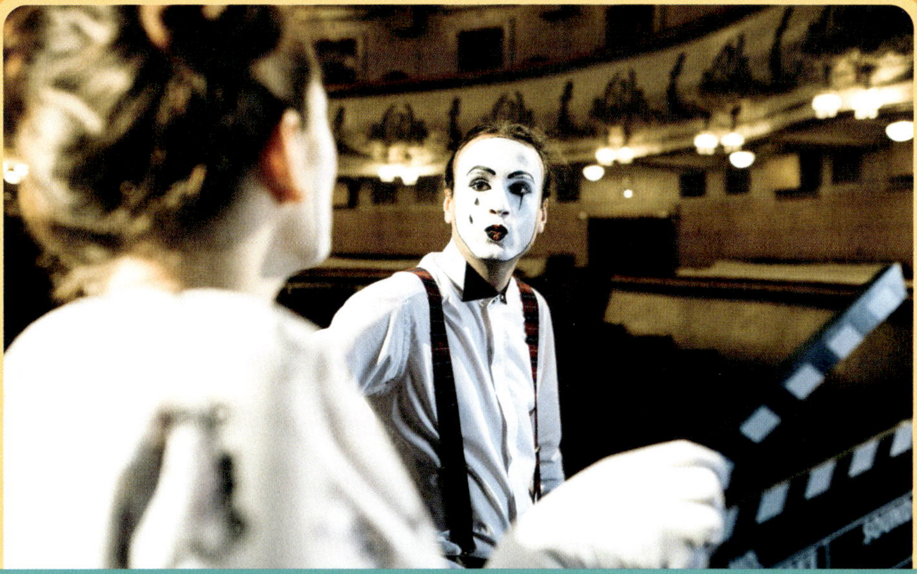

Learning Film-Related Skills

The following classes are available at many middle and high schools. Each one can be useful for a student interested in filmmaking.

- Art
- Computer science
- Creative writing
- Music
- Photography
- Theater

CHAPTER ONE

"Are you sure?" Raven looked at the phone Josh held in his hand. "I bet you have a lot of videos in there."

Josh frowned. "That's not the same thing."

A woman came up behind them. "Oh, good!" she said to herself as she picked up the film and video class sheet. "We have lots of future filmmakers."

"Are you the instructor?" Raven asked her. "I can't wait to start."

"Yes, I'm Ms. Chen," the woman answered, "and I'm so glad you're excited for the class. How about you?" she asked Josh.

"He has the best story ideas," Raven told Ms. Chen.

"I do have a story idea I want to work on," Josh admitted.

"Terrific!" said Ms. Chen. "Sounds like you're already off to a great start. Today is all about selecting an idea. Then we will start creating **storyboards**."

Another Form of Storytelling

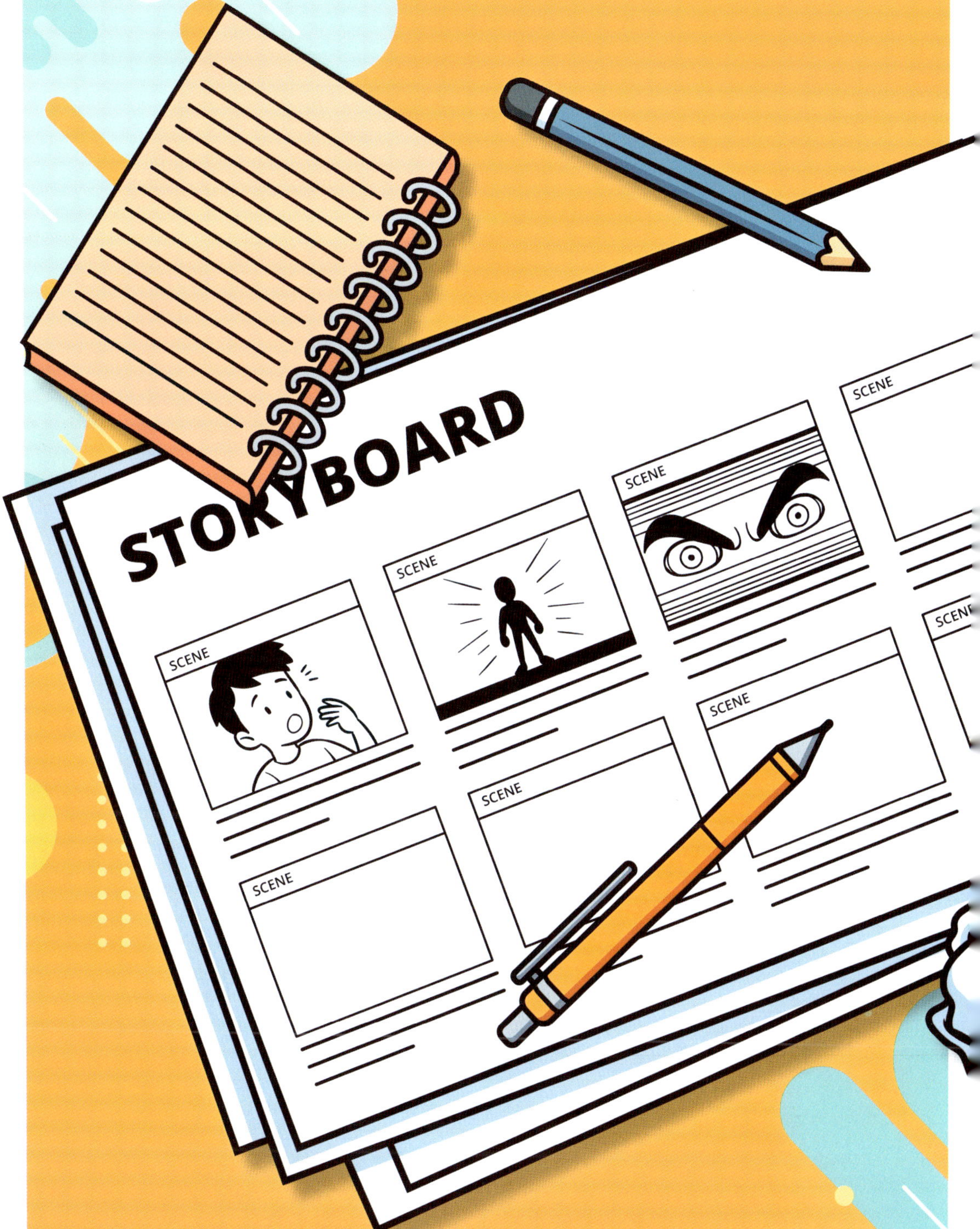

CHAPTER ONE

Raven bounced on her toes. "What do you think, Josh?"

He shoved his phone back in his pocket and signed the sheet. He decided to give the film and video class a try. His graphic novel idea would make a cool movie. The more he thought about it, the more thrilling it sounded.

Later that afternoon, Josh climbed into his father's truck. "How is the graphic novel coming along?" his dad asked.

"That class was full," Josh explained. "But I signed up for a different one."

"That's too bad," his dad answered. "I know you were looking forward to working on your idea."

"I still get to," Josh said, and then added, "I'm learning how to make films." Raven had been right. There was more than one way to tell a story. Josh couldn't wait for tomorrow. He didn't need a mysterious book to tell him that the next day was going to be fun. He already knew it would be, because he'd get to start writing the script for his own film. "When we get home, I'll show you my storyboard," he told his father.

Another Form of Storytelling

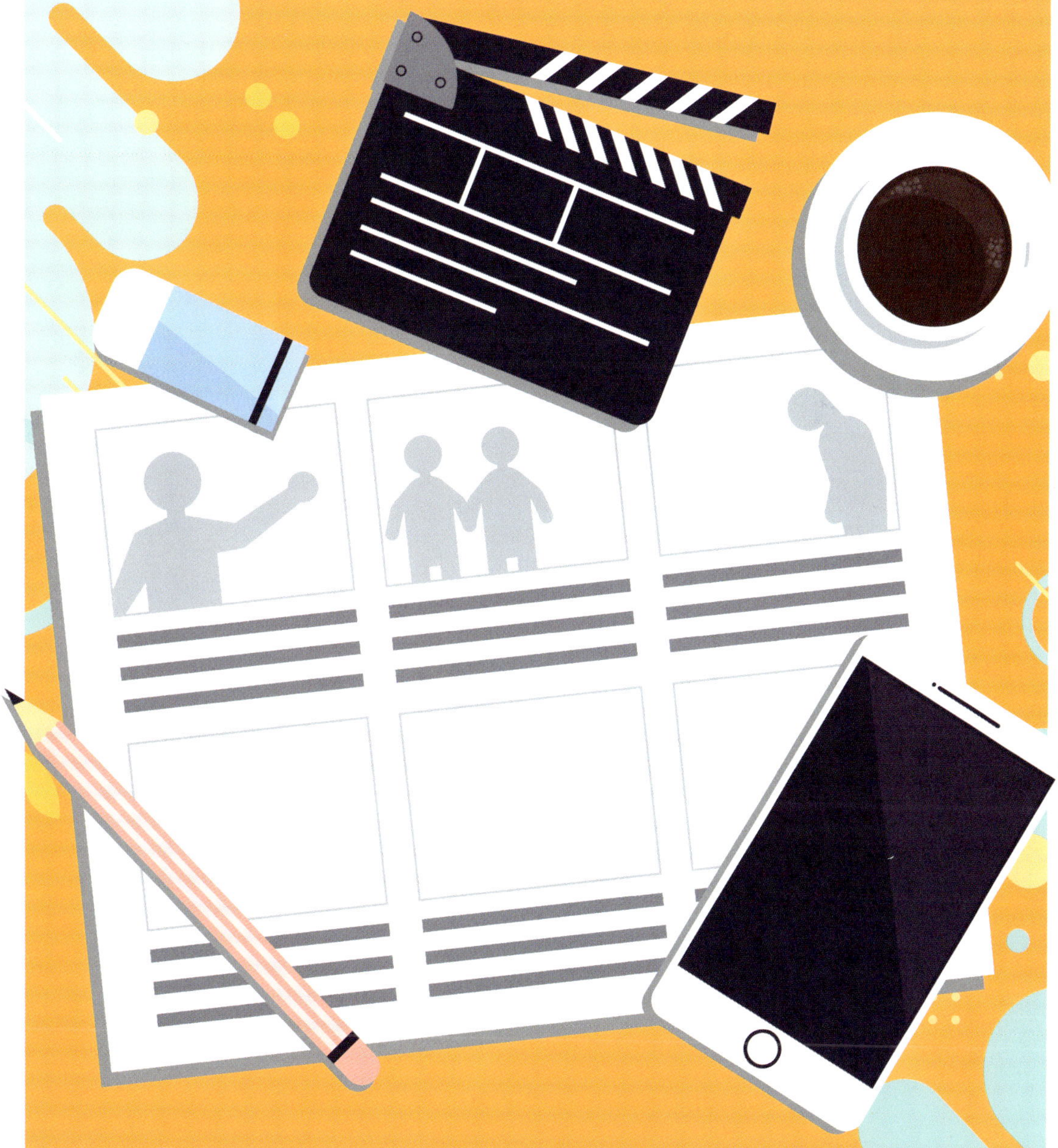

Chapter Two

More Than a Century of Filmmaking

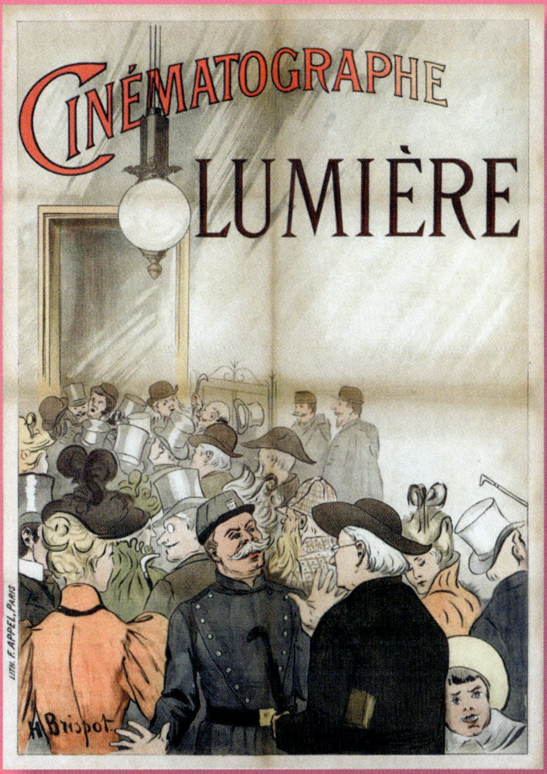

In 1895, excited audience members sat in their seats in a theater in Paris, France, as the screen blazed to light. The Lumiere brothers had invented the Cinématographe. Their new machine was a camera, as well as a projector. Using their invention, they thrilled the audience with a series of ten short films. None was more than one minute long. But these recordings began paving the way for future films and videos, and the many people who now create them.

CHAPTER TWO

Film and video-making is the process of creating a movie from beginning to end. This process is divided into three basic parts. The first is called preproduction. During this phase, a writer turns an idea into a script. A cast and film crew are also chosen. Next is the production phase. During this phase of the project, filming sites are found, and all the film's scenes are shot. The third and final phase is postproduction. This is when the audio and video will be edited. Special effects, such as computer-generated imagery (CGI), are also added during this phase. CGI is the technology that created the dinosaurs in Steven Spielberg's *Jurassic Park* series.

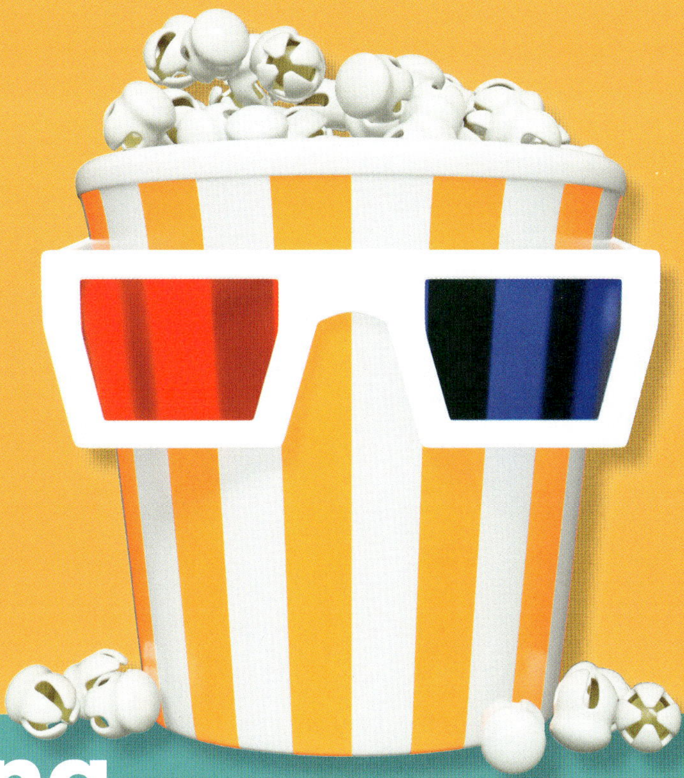

Going Three-Dimensional

In the 1950s, movie producers worried that the popularity of television would lower movie attendance. To spark more interest, some filmmakers began shooting movies, such as *The House of Wax* and *The Creature from the Black Lagoon*, in 3D. This format makes certain objects look like they are jumping off the screen toward viewers. 3D films are still popular today.

CHAPTER TWO

Spielberg was born in 1946. He began shooting his own films as a teenager. He made his first feature-length film, *Firelight*, when he was just sixteen years old. But it was a movie about a shark that made Spielberg famous in the film industry. His 1975 movie *Jaws* earned more than $470 million. It also won three Academy Awards.

People all over the world have seen Spielberg's movies—such as *The Goonies*, *Ready Player One*, and the *Indiana Jones* series. Many of the scenes in his movies were inspired by things that scared Spielberg as a child. As a toddler, he was afraid of a twisted tree in his yard. He turned to this fear while creating his 1982 movie *Poltergeist*.

"[The tree] looked like arms and long fingers and long fingernails," he told Terry Gross on *Fresh Air*, "and later, as an adult, when I wrote *Poltergeist*, I created a tree out the window that actually comes to life and grabs a kid and starts to suck him into one of its knotholes." Making movies has been a way for Spielberg to deal with his fears. "I was afraid of the dark. I was afraid of small places and I still am today." But now, he turns those fears into art.

More Than a Century of Filmmaking

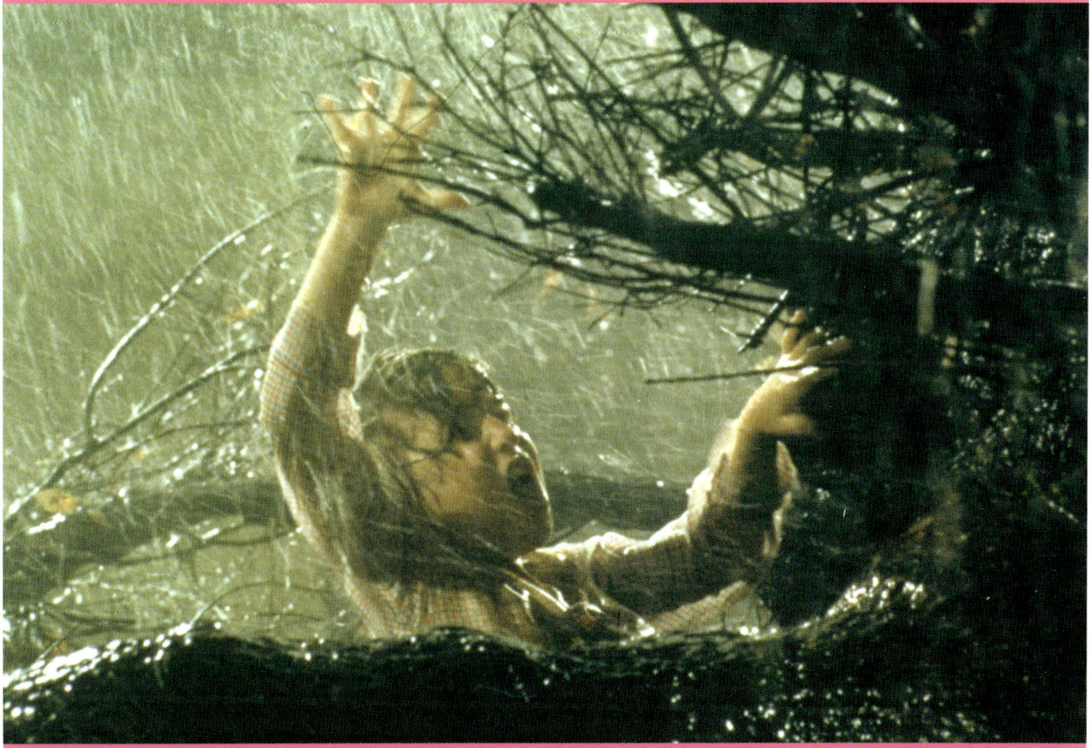

The tree scene in *Poltergeist* was filmed in reverse to make it seem as though the actor was pulled into the tree.

CHAPTER TWO

Filmmaker Greta Gerwig is one of only five women to be **nominated** for Best Director in the history of the Academy Awards. Gerwig was already known for films such as 2017's *Lady Bird* and 2019's *Little Women*. Then she released *Barbie* in 2023. She both directed and cowrote the film, which made more than $626 million. When asked how she came to make a movie about a toy, Gerwig told *Time* magazine she had always loved dolls. "I played with dolls too long. I was still doing it in junior high."

Gerwig has advice for young people who want to get into **screenwriting**. "Write, write, write as much as you can," she said at the Jabob Burns Film Center in Pleasantville, New York. "Then shoot on a phone. I've seen great films made that way," she added.

More Than a Century of Filmmaking

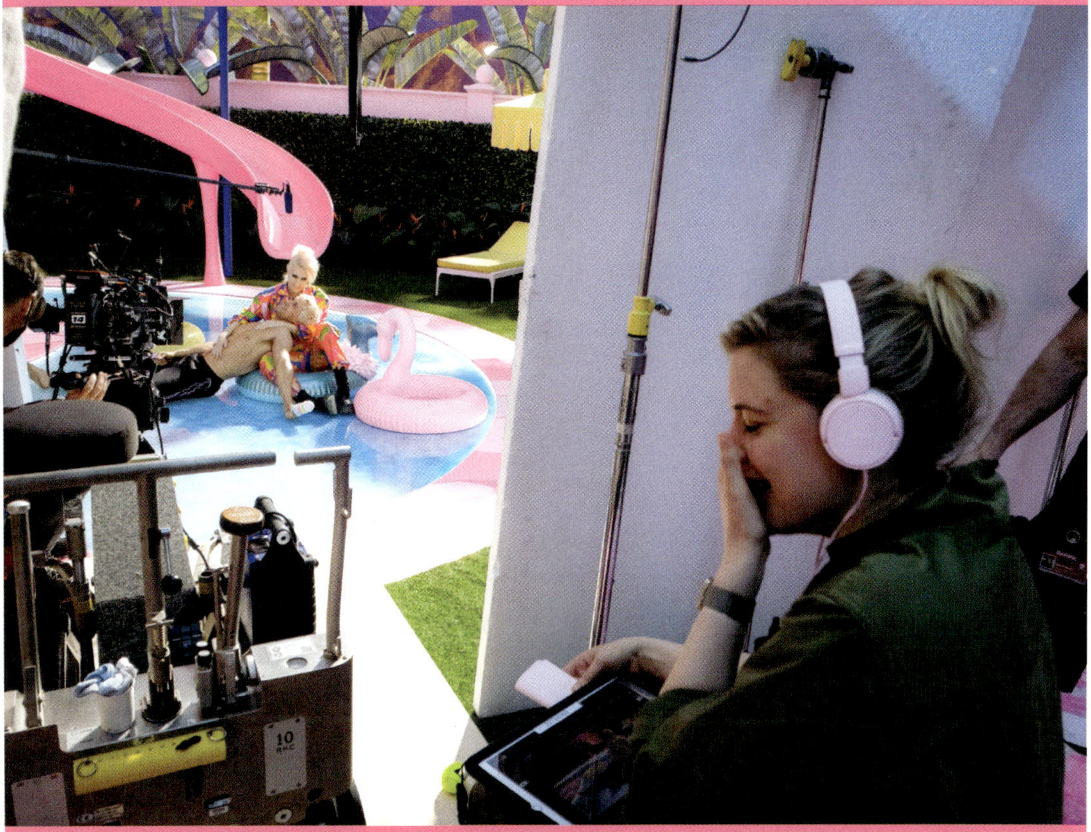

Gerwig was inspired by 33 separate movies, including *The Wizard of Oz* and *Close Encounters of the Third Kind*, when creating *Barbie*.

Chapter Three

One Film, Many Jobs

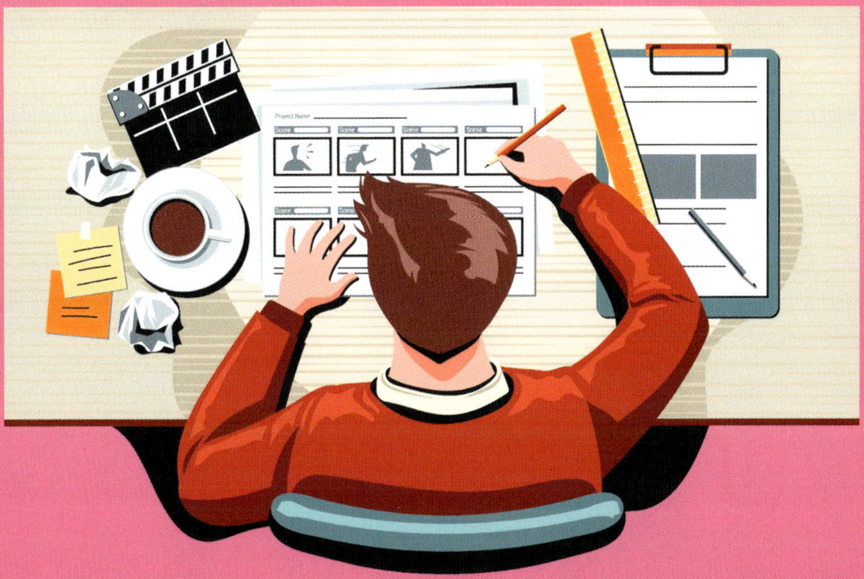

There are many ways to work in filmmaking. One is screenwriting. A screenplay, which a screenwriter creates, is like a blueprint for a movie. It contains character descriptions, **dialogue**, and details about the movie's settings. Screenwriters need plenty of imagination. They must turn their ideas into plots.

CHAPTER THREE

A college degree isn't required to become a screenwriter. But attending a film program teaches important subjects such as creative writing, film theory, and screenwriting itself. David Nathan Weiss is a screenwriter known for movies such as *Shrek* and *All Dogs Go to Heaven*. He told the *Raindance* website the steps he took before attending the University of Southern California's School of Cinematic Arts. "I always wanted to put on a show. I was in theater constantly, in plays, producing plays, in the talent show. . . . Dancing, singing, running the light board, acting, it was just in my blood."

One Film, Many Jobs

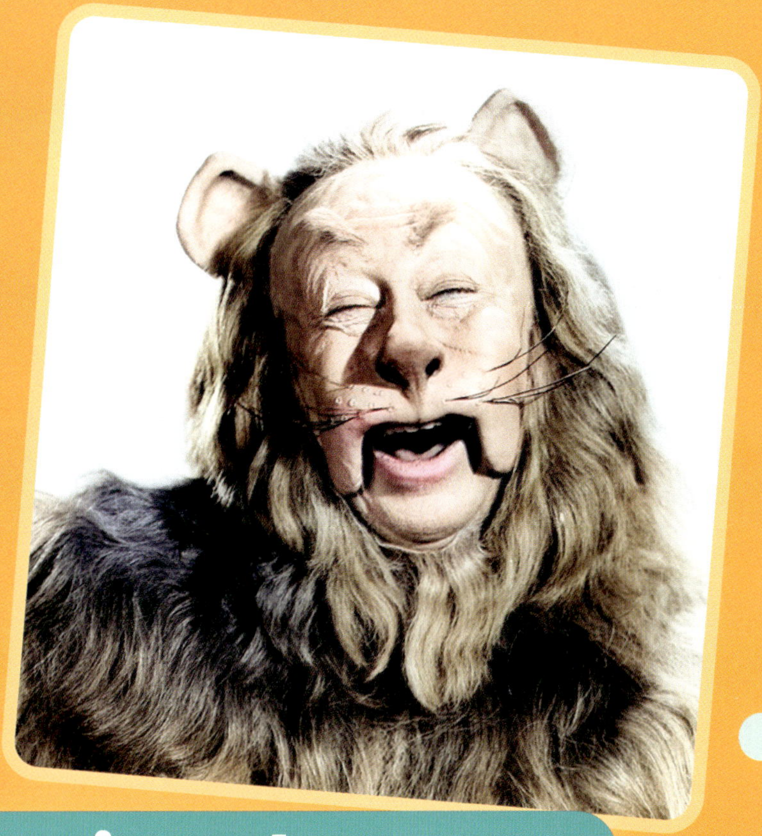

Dressing the Part

Costume design is more than deciding what outfits actors wear. Clothing sets the mood of a scene and helps define characters. Costumes are an important storytelling tool. One of the most **iconic** movie costumes of the twentieth century is the Cowardly Lion from *The Wizard of Oz*. In 2014, this character's costume sold at an auction for more than $3 million.

CHAPTER THREE

A movie's director oversees the filming of a project. Directors work closely with other people on the set such as the cast, the lighting crew, and the camera crew. After filming, directors also work closely with the film editor in postproduction. Directors are involved in a film from beginning to end.

In addition to being creative, directors need good communication skills. They need to make sure the cast and crew all understand the director's vision for the film. Directors need strong leadership skills. It's their job to unite everyone on the film set.

One Film, Many Jobs

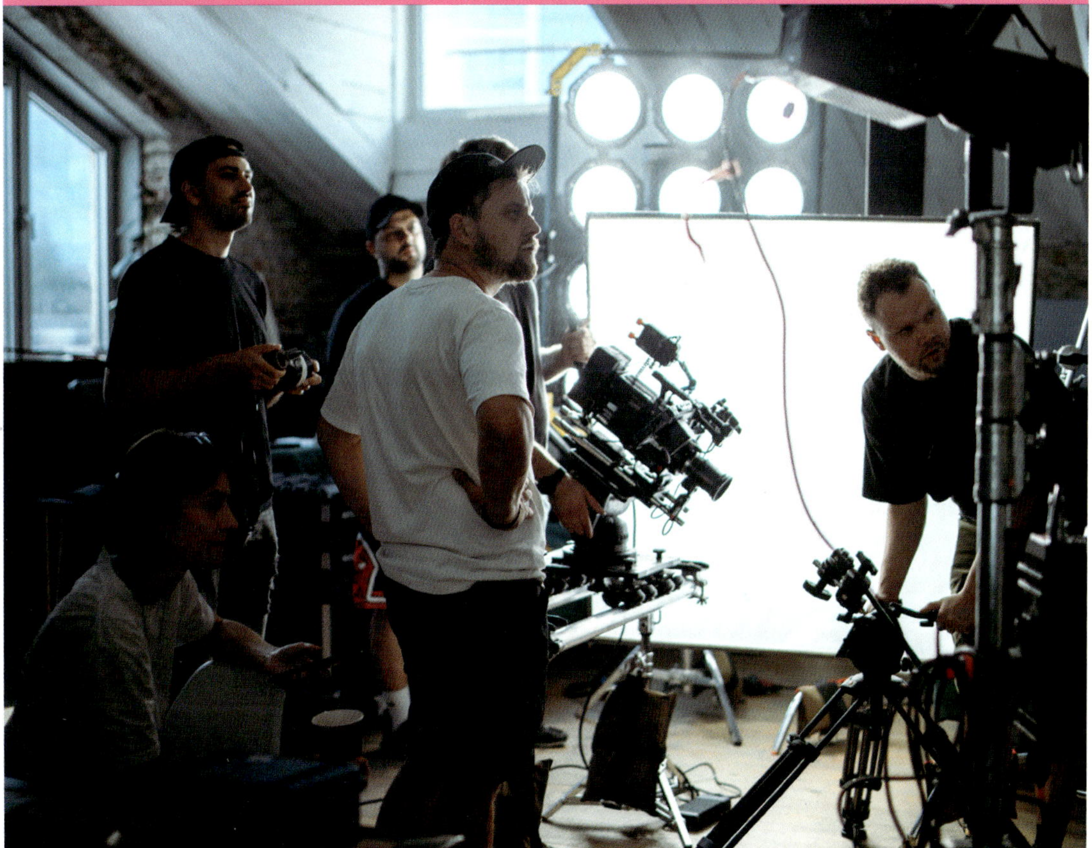

Crews on set waiting for the next shot

CHAPTER THREE

Craig Johnson directed *The Skeleton Twins* and Netflix's *Alex Strangelove*. He talked to the *Lunacy U* website about the importance of people skills. "Your job often as a director is making everybody on set feel like their job is the most important. So that's the costume designer. That's the director of photography. That's your producers. That's the actors." But sometimes emotions can get heated. "I've been frustrated," Johnson admitted. "But you take a deep breath, you go walk off set, you scream at a brick wall, you kick a can, you yell privately."

One Film, Many Jobs

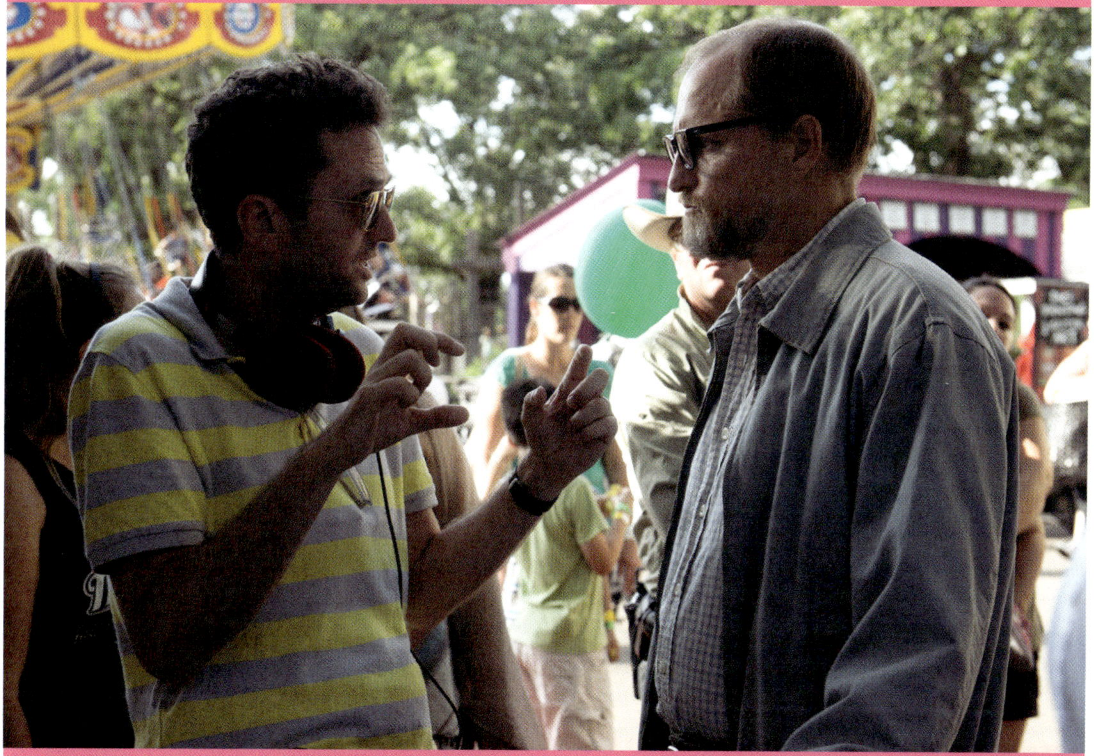

Craig Johnson offers feedback to actor Woody Harrelson on the set of the 2017 film *Wilson*.

CHAPTER THREE

Camera operators are responsible for filming the movie. They make sure all the equipment is in working order, the lenses are clean, and the batteries are charged. Camera operators work closely with the director. Most camera operators have a bachelor's degree, which takes about four years to earn. But some go into the field with a two-year associate's degree. Other camera operators attend workshops, complete **internships**, or work as **apprentices** before getting a job.

One Film, Many Jobs

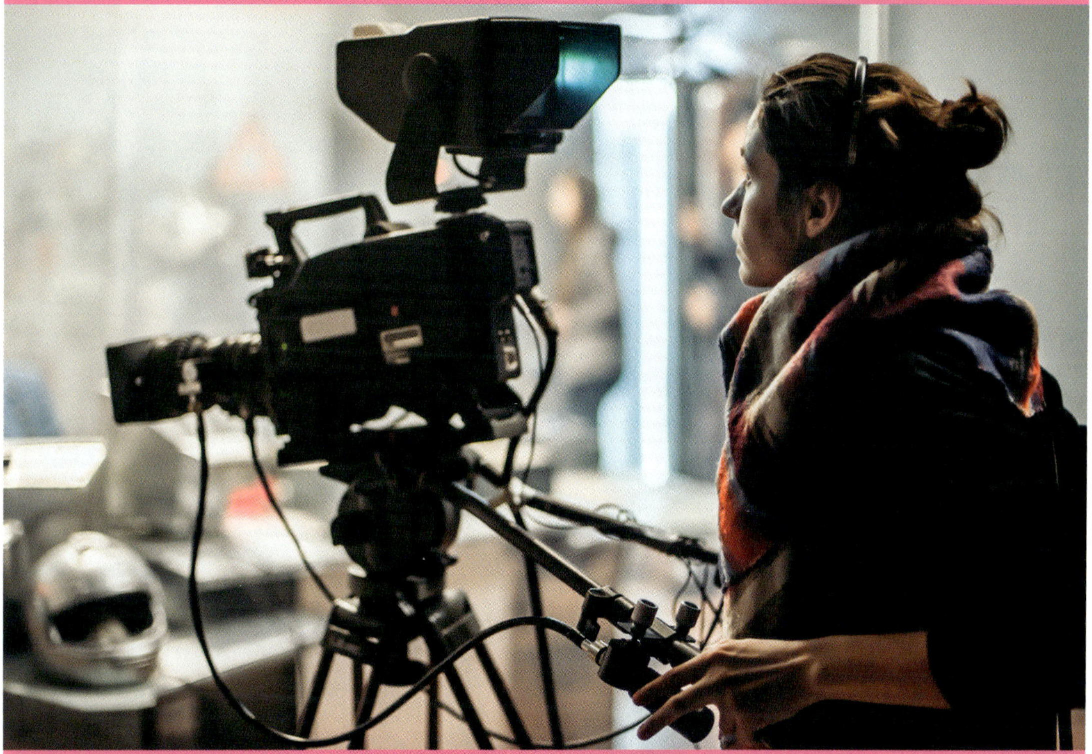

A camera operator looks through the optical viewfinder during a shoot.

Chapter Four

Long Hours on the Set

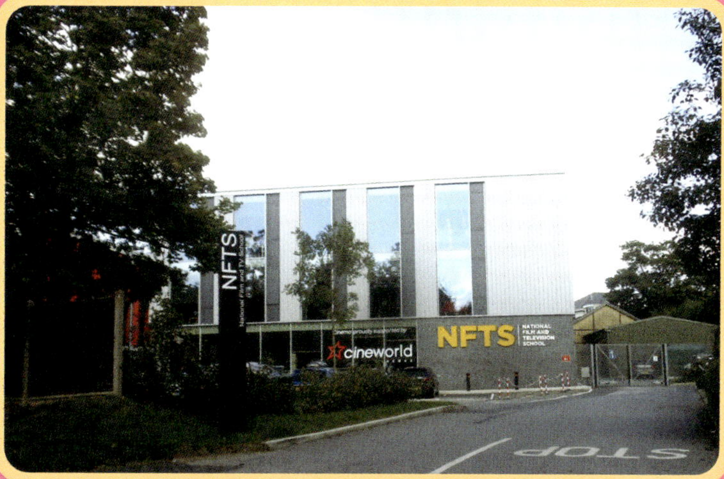

The National Film and Television School was established as the National Film School in 1971.

Writer, director, and filmmaker Benjamin Hunter is a graduate of the National Film and Television School in the United Kingdom. His work has been honored multiple times at the Royal Television Society Awards. After finishing his education, Hunter found that the professional world wasn't an easy one. He faced a lot of rejection. "The reality is there is a lot of competition in the industry, and even if you are incredible at what you do, you will **inevitably** often lose pitches," he told the *InvestIN* website. But he also pointed out that there are many opportunities out there. Hunter thinks that for people with a thick skin who work hard, the effort can pay off.

CHAPTER FOUR

Hunter's days vary greatly. Shooting films, writing, **networking**, and researching take up most of his time. He also spends hours reading screenplays and watching films to improve his own craft. When Hunter is filming, it often means long hours on the set. A twelve-hour day is usually the minimum. Some film crews work sixteen-hour days. Hunter keeps his crew's hours shorter. "My goal is to make the same level of quality films and still treat my crew members with the respect they deserve, by giving them time off," he told *Shout Out Colorado*.

Filmmaker Tom Antos has worked on both small, independent films and large Hollywood productions. Like Hunter, a day for Antos can vary. He spends some days travelling to work on a shoot. When he's working from his home office, he starts his day off with exercise such as running or yoga to clear his mind. Then he's on to what he calls "boring work"—checking emails and social media. After that, he moves on to editing existing video or filming for a new project. "Most of the time," Antos says in a video on his website, "I have multiple projects going on at the same time."

Long Hours on the Set

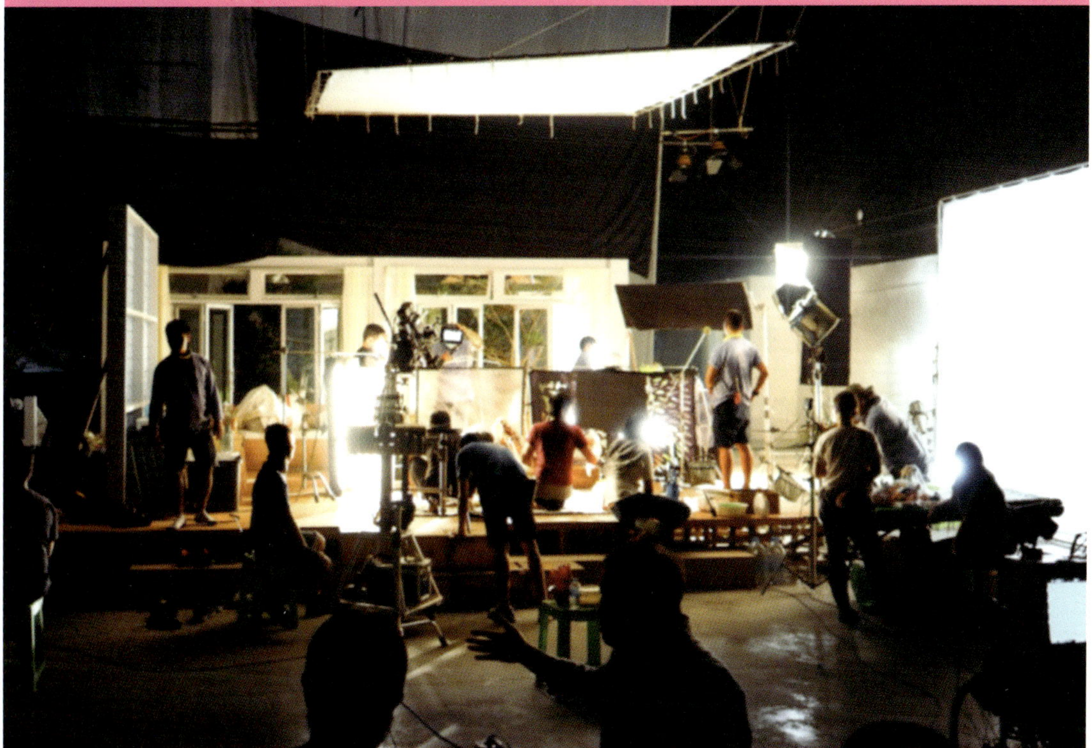

Actors and crews working to set up a scene

CHAPTER FOUR

Creating a film costs a lot of money. Even a small film can cost between $10,000 and $100,000. The independent horror film *The Blair Witch Project* cost $60,000 to make in 1999. Bigger movies cost much more. The 2024 Marvel movie *Deadpool & Wolverine* had a budget of $200 million. A big part of a filmmaker's job is finding funding. Some filmmakers use their own money. Others **crowdsource** or write **grants** to fund their projects.

Another way to get funding is pitching the idea to investors. A pitch is a short description of the project made to convince an investor to provide funding. Effective pitches must show a clear vision for the project. Investors are looking for a return on their money. It is part of the filmmaker's job to show that there's an audience out there who will pay to see the movie the filmmaker plans to make.

Long Hours on the Set

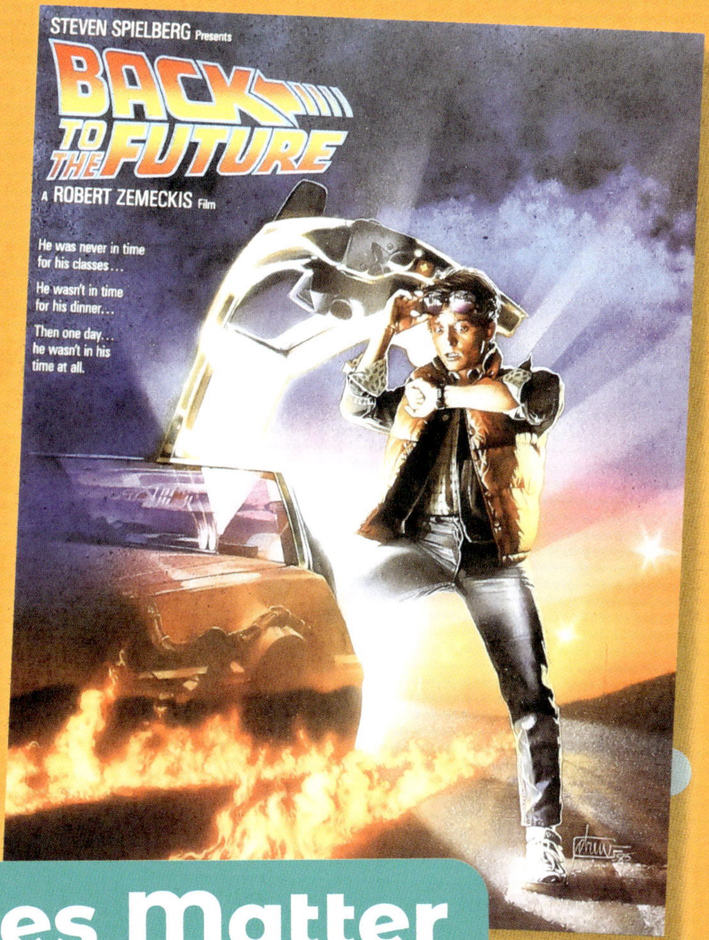

Titles Matter

Many people have never heard of the movie *Space Man from Pluto*. But they are familiar with a film called *Back to the Future*. Even with Steven Spielberg involved, the idea for *Back to the Future* was rejected forty times before the project was funded. With its updated title, the film was finally made and became the most popular movie of 1985. It is still popular on streaming services today.

Chapter Five

Making Something Happen

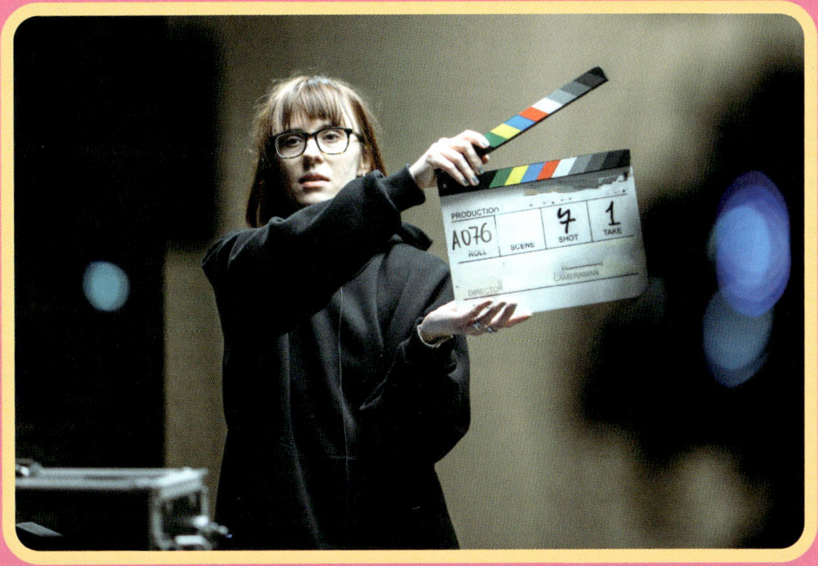

Working in the film and video industry is a creative and exciting career choice. But it is also highly **competitive**. About fifty thousand students graduate with degrees related to this industry each year. Many other people come to filmmaking with a two-year communications degree. Still others have no college education at all. Most people who work on scripted films are freelancers. This means they take short-term jobs, making a living one project at a time. A career in filmmaking often means facing rejection. Despite these challenges, the appeal of working in film and video is still strong.

CHAPTER FIVE

There are many paths to success in filmmaking. Young people interested in this career should take advantage of classes that focus on writing, video production, and technology. Sign up for language arts classes and explore creative writing. Take art and computer courses. Get involved in school and community theater.

Filmmaker Martin Scorsese stresses the importance of watching movies, a lot of movies. "You need to study movies in order to make movies. Watch the good ones, the bad ones, and the amazing ones. Figure out what makes them tick," he said in an interview with the *Medium* website.

Attending film festivals is a great way to see a wide range of movies. It may not be possible to attend the largest of these events, such as the Cannes Film Festival in France or the Venice Film Festival in Italy. But local film festivals often show some of the same movies. These smaller events may also include films by independent filmmakers who are just getting their start in the business.

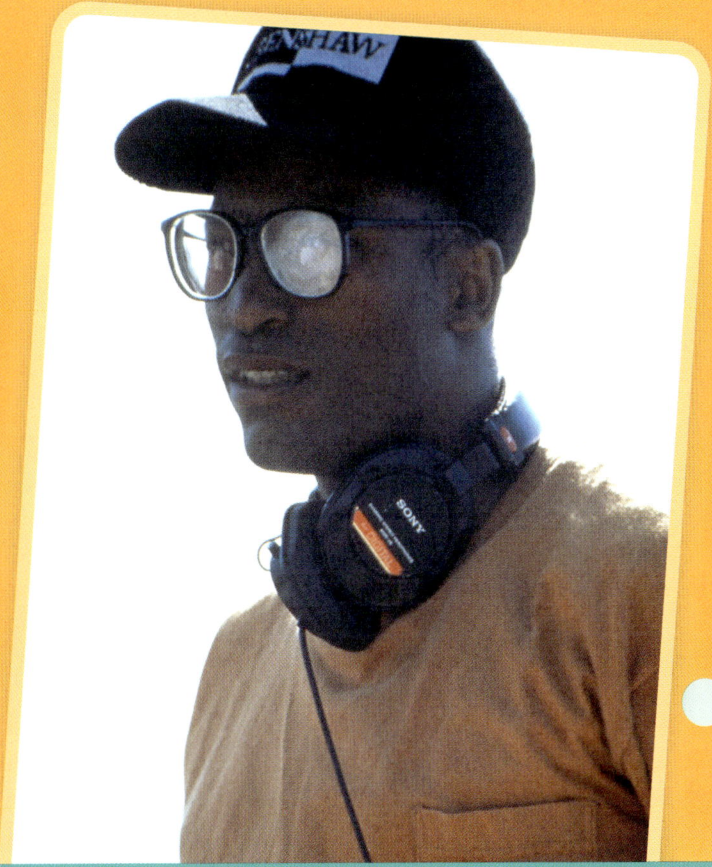

Lights, Camera, History!

The youngest director to be nominated for an Oscar is John Singleton. An Oscar is the nickname for the Academy Award. Singleton was twenty-four when his 1991 film *Boyz n the Hood* received the nod from the Academy of Motion Picture Arts and Sciences. It also made him the first Black director to be nominated for an Oscar.

CHAPTER FIVE

The FutureWave Shorts Competition is part of the Seattle International Film Festival. Each May, the festival spotlights young filmmakers and awards the Wavemaker Award for Excellence in Youth Filmmaking. Other cities that host youth film festivals include Austin, Texas; Boston, Massachusetts; Indianapolis, Indiana; and Los Angeles, California.

Isaiah Brody was seventeen years old when he made his first feature film. *The Last Night in the Life of Death* was an official selection at the Mammoth Lakes Film Festival in California. In an interview with the *GabFest* website, he told young people, "Practice, practice, practice. Just go out and make something happen, go have fun. My best friend Max and I made over 100 short films before we even graduated middle school." He shared that most of them were filmed with their parents' iPhones. "That was really good practice for the future."

Making Something Happen

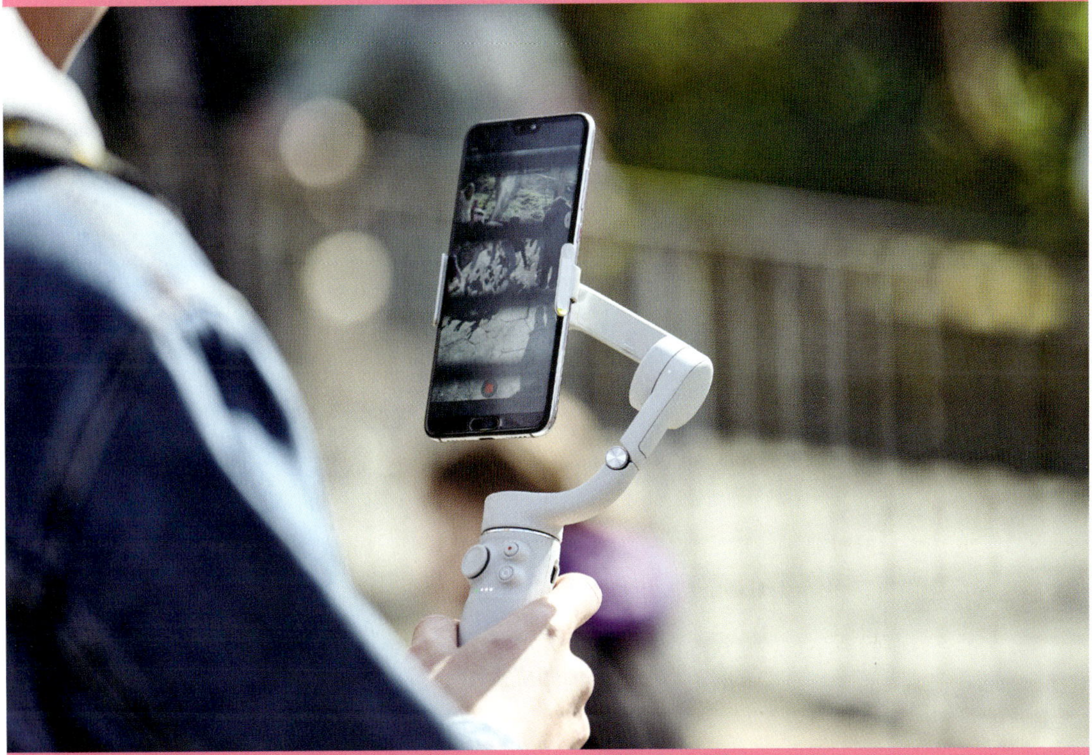

Filmmaking software and apps aid in creating films on smartphones.

CHAPTER FIVE

Benjamin Hunter thinks smartphones are an excellent way to get started in film. "Everyone has a camera phone in their pocket," he tells *InvestIN*. "Make little films with your friends and family, or with the network you are slowly expanding. Learn from your mistakes and learn the craft of filmmaking. Then, once you start making things you're proud of, your network will be there to get that thing out into the world and hopefully get the ball rolling on your career!"

Making Something Happen

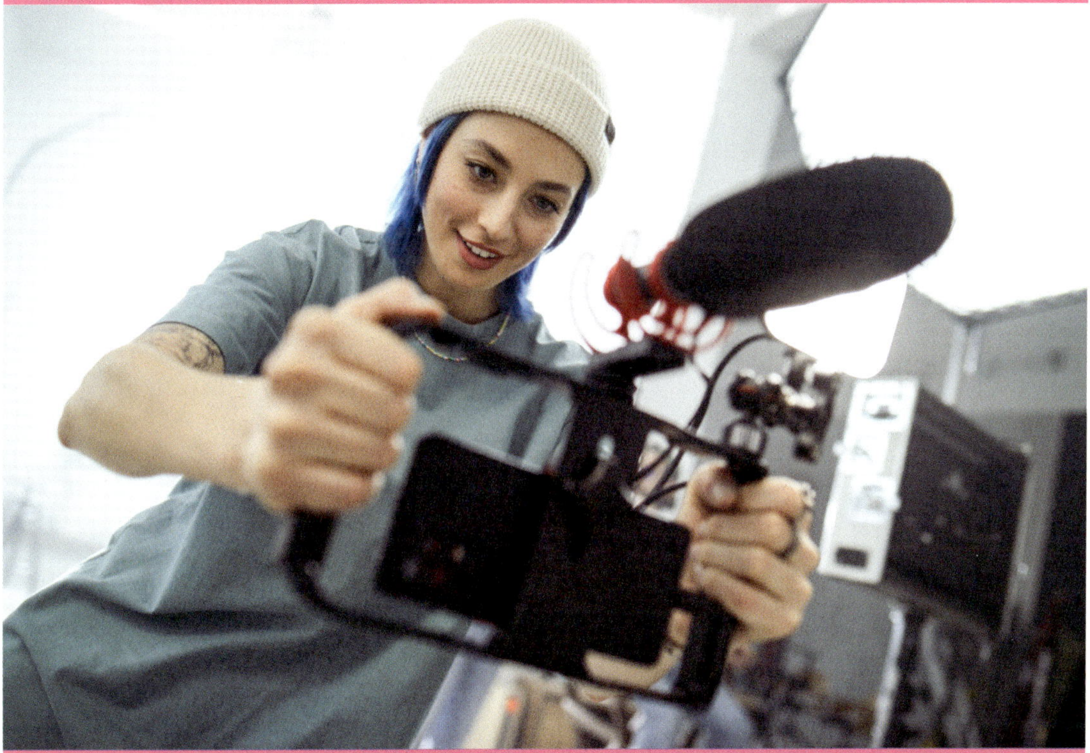

A student filmmaker uses audio and visual equipment in a studio.

Glossary

apprentices
People who work for another person to learn a skill or trade

competitive
Related to going up against others in a challenge

crowdsource
Ask for online donations for a specific goal, such as making a movie

dialogue
Words spoken by a character

grants
Gifts of money for a particular purpose

iconic
Well established and widely recognized

inevitably
Occurring in a way that cannot be avoided

internships
Jobs given to students for the purpose of gaining skills and experience

networking
Interacting with others to create business connections

nominated
Named as a candidate for an award or honor

screenwriting
The act of creating a film script

storyboards
Series of drawings that show the plot of films

Ready, Set, Action!

Test your new knowledge of filmmaking by answering the following questions.

1. A series of drawings that show the plot for a film is called a:

- **A.** Graphic novel
- **B.** Storyboard
- **C.** Cinématographe

2. Steven Spielberg used a tree from his childhood as inspiration for the film:

- **A.** *Poltergeist*
- **B.** *The Goonies*
- **C.** *Back to the Future*

3. What level of education do most camera operators have?

- **A.** No college
- **B.** An associate's degree
- **C.** A bachelor's degree

4. How much did the film *Deadpool & Wolverine* cost to make?

- **A.** $60,000
- **B.** $100,000
- **C.** $200 million

Answers: B, A, C, C

Find Out More

IN PRINT

Fredeen, Kerry Kelaher. *A Career in Animation*. Mitchell Lane Publishers, 2026.

Greenspan, Judy. *Steven Spielberg: Get to Know the Extraordinary Filmmaker*. Capstone Press, 2020.

Owen, Ruth and Willis, John. *CGI Artists*. AV2, 2020.

ON THE INTERNET

International High School Film & Screenwriting Contest.
https://filmfreeway.com/IHSSC

Script Slug.
www.scriptslug.com

"Youth Programs," ***Film Independent*, n.d.**
www.filmindependent.org/programs/youth-programs

Index

About the Author

Author Nancy Coffelt loves watching movies on rainy days. Her favorites are classic horror films such as *Frankenstein* and *The Blob*. Nancy also wrote *A Career in Architectural Design* and *A Career in Fashion Design* for this book series.